Aunty M Aunty M Aunty M Aunty M
Aunty M Aunty Aunty M Aunty
Aunty M Aunty M Aunty M
Aunty M Aunty M Aunty M Aunty M Aunty
Aunty M Aunty M Aunty M Aunty M
Aunty M Aunty M Aunty M Aunty M Aunty
Aunty M Aunty M Aunty M Aunty M
Aunty M Aunty M Aunty M Aunty M Aunty
Aunty M Aunty M Aunty M Aunty M
Aunty M Aunty M Aunty M Aunty M Aunty
Aunty M Aunty M Aunty M Aunty M
Aunty M Aunty M Aunty M Aunty M Aunty
Aunty M Aunty M Aunty M Aunty M
Aunty M Aunty M Aunty M Aunty M Aunty
Aunty M Aunty M Aunty M Aunty M

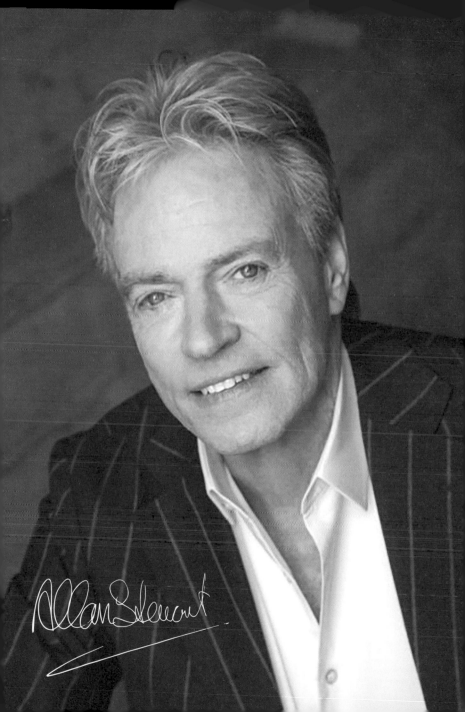

For **Jane, Kate, and David,**
who all put up with my sense
of humour.

I love you soooooooo much.

Written and illustrated by **Allan Stewart**

Foreword written by **Ross King MBE**

Edited by **Susan Cohen** with artistic assistance
from **Jane Cornwell**

Proofread by **Angus Stewart**

A CIP record of this book is available from the British Library.

Hardback ISBN **978-1-913237-04-2**

Printed by **Bell & Bain Ltd.**

First published in the UK by The Wee Book Company Ltd, 2019.

www.theweebookcompany.com

Foreword by Ross King MBE

(Good Morning Britain's Hollywood correspondent)

I've known Aunty May through her nephew, my best pal Allan Stewart, for most of my life - that's thirty-five years in showbiz years and fifty in real ones.

I love that fact that Allan has always loved his Aunty so much, it even looks like he's turning into her. Mind you, back in the day, Allan would only wear a dress at weekends.

I first met Allan when I was a schoolboy ... s-t-e-a-d-y ... when I went to see his 'hit' (I think that's how you spell it) TV show in the dear old STV studios in the Coocaddens. I genuinely loved watching him in full flow - a man of a thousand voices, most of them sounding the same. After that we became fast friends, and to this day I refer to him as the big brother I never wanted.

Now that I look back, we got up to some mischief! I remember one time, after we'd been to Charlie Parker's, we went back to Aunty May's and started making a noise well into the wee sma' hours in the room next to hers. She shouted to us, 'have you boys got strong drink in there?' 'No!' we shouted back together, in unison, both at the same time - things are always funnier in threes. Next thing we knew, May had opened the door and thrown in a bottle of Bell's.

I was lucky in that May was always there with good advice.

I once asked her what I should get Allan for his birthday, since he had everything. She answered, 'if he's got everything give him penicillin.'

Ahhh, and I'll never forget May passing on some sage showbiz advice to me when I was just starting out - the very same advice she'd given to Allan, which has stood him in good stead to this day … 'Start at the bottom,' she said, '… and kiss it!'

I could tell how much May loved her husband Hector by the way she constantly put him down. She said that she'd tried to put Hector into an Ugly Competition, but he was rejected as they didn't accept professionals.

Then there was that time at Edinburgh Zoo when she walked up to a member of staff and said, 'take a good look at my Hector. I know you're stock-taking and I don't want any arguments on the way out!'

Mind you, way before she met Hector, I've heard that May was a bit of a gal! She'd had a boyfriend who worked at the zoo. I don't know what became of him, but she swore he was a keeper.

I now live in L.A. but that hasn't kept me and Allan apart. We still keep in touch. May, who's always kept up with the latest trends, told us that there's a great way to communicate on Scottish Social Media - it's called You Ya-tube.

Distance has never come between me and May either. She's always liked to travel, and years ago she and Hector visited me in Hollywood. She said it was so lovely to see so many new faces - mainly on the old ones.

I've been lucky enough to catch up with May on a few cruises too. Mind you, wherever we meet up – on sea or on land – she always makes me laugh.

'Hello, son,' she always says, 'you get your good looks from your father. He was a Beverly Hills plastic surgeon, wasn't he?'

I make a point of going to see her in panto whenever I can. I love it when Allan asks her where she reckons his career's going. She always replies, 'it's behind you!'

Joking aside, May is one of the most wonderful ladies I've ever met. She's warm, cuddly, full of life, and I'm proud to call her my Aunty too.

Sometimes I'll say to Allan, 'I wish you were more like your Aunty May.' It's funny, but his reply is always the sume: 'I'm a lot more like her than you'll ever know.'

DEAR AUNTY MAY

Selected Letters To Edinburgh's Favourite Agony Aunt

Well, hello there! Aunty May here - woman of the world, friend of the people, and the Edinburgh Bugle's long-standing Agony Aunt.

I've been receiving letters from poor troubled souls at my desk at the Edinburgh Bugle HQ for many years now (well, I say 'HQ' but it's more of a walk-in cupboard with a kettle in the corner). You'll find me there, slaving away on my correspondence on a Tuesday morning before Zumba and a Thursday afternoon after choir practice. I'm very dedicated.

Yes, I've lived life to the full and I'm still firing on all cylinders. There's life in this old Morningside girl yet! I bring a wealth of life experience to my weekly column and I trust you'll think it shows.

I'd like to think I understand my fellow Scots pretty well and I've always been happy to give folk the benefit of my opinion. Goodness, I remember way back when I was a wee girl of eleven years old at Bruntsfield Primary School, my teacher Miss Anderson asked me if I liked her dress. 'I love the material,' I said, 'I see you sold the caravan and kept the curtains!' She wasnae happy.

I've always been sought out as a confidante and problem solver. It's just my lot in life. Just like everybody else, the family lean on me too. For instance, my Wee Allan (my nephew, the entertainer Allan Stewart – you might know him) has always rung me up to ask my opinion. I remember way back when he used to have problems with his love life. 'It's a minefield,' I used to say to him, 'so sail your course steady, cap'n!' Sure enough he did, good lad. He found a wonderful girl and has been happily married for over thirty years.

I was pretty good at sailing a steady course too and found a safe harbour with my late husband, Hector. Sadly, he's gone to the big soccer pitch in the sky ... he loved football. He was a wonderful man and I do miss him. At home it's just me and my wee Cockapoo, Mini May, now. Some people say we are starting to look alike.

Still, I have a wide circle of friends, what with my Zumba classes, my choir practice and my origami group. My oldest friend Maggie has stuck by me through thick and thin, though. She was thick and I was thin. Oh, and I've decided to get out there again and have been dating. Well, I've just had the odd wee night oot - very odd. I'll tell you more about that later.

Of course, what keeps me really busy is my performance in the King's Panto. I l-o-v-e it. Mind you, it takes so much out of me. I'm getting on, you know – I'm sixty plus VAT Still, I take it easy for the rest of the year.

Ma wee Maggie

You see, I like to take a wee holiday here and there, and I do like a nice cruise. Hector and I loved going on our holidays but he would never go on cruises with me because he got sea sick. I once said to him, 'aren't you worried that I might cheat on you when I'm away at sea? You'd better come with me to make sure I don't!' He looked at me and said, 'I'd rather you cheated!'

It's funny. I'm always answering other people's questions, yet I have so many of my own. For instance, why do the shoes you are wearing suddenly look so old when you go into the shop to try on new ones? Why do men's toilets smell worse than women's toilets? (Don't ask me how I know that!) Why do they have a sign saying, 'Weak Bridge'? Does that mean that if you go on the bridge and it collapses they can say, 'well, we did warn you'? Oh, the burden of an enquiring mind!

Well, that's enough of me for noo. Here are a few letters from my weekly column over the years which have stuck out in my memory. I hope they whet your appetite for our beloved Edinburgh Bugle. Before you know it, you might be following my column every week! Now, wouldn't that just be the very dab?

I should tell you that I've changed the names to protect the innocent, or is it the guilty? I've also included some of my musings about life. As you may know, they're much sought after.

Love,

Aunty M

HOME COMFORTS

Dear Aunty May

I love my garden but my topiary is getting to be quite unruly. How do you deal with this?

Dermot

Dear Dermot

I like it all au naturel. I won't let anyone trim my bush.

Aunty M

MY TOPIARY
(WHAT DID YOU
THINK I MEANT)

Dear Aunty May

I'm a 68 year old woman. I love my home, I love nature, and I have never so much as killed a fly, so imagine how upset I was this morning when I was in the shower and washed a spider down the plug hole. I feel so guilty!

Kate

Dear Kate

Don't feel guilty. The spider probably took one look at your naked body and leapt willingly down the plug hole to its death.

Oh! No offence.

Aunty M

When I'm at home, I sometimes get strange 'phone calls. One day, a lady with a foreign accent asked if I'd had an accident recently. I said yes, I had, but how did she know? She said she was from a claims company and they know these things. She asked if it was serious. I said yes, it was to me. She asked me for the details because she said she could get me some compensation.

I told her that when I went to the theatre to see Michael McIntyre. I thought he was the funniest comedian I'd ever seen, and I laughed so much that I wet myself.

She asked, 'so when did you have the accident?' I replied, 'I've just told you – I wet myself!' She hung up.

Dear Aunty May

I have seen a lot of adverts lately for walk-in baths.
What do you think of them?

Cheryl

Dear Cheryl

**I've seen those adverts as
well, but I can't work them
out. Surely when you open
the door all the water
pours out?**

Aunty M

I went shopping a wee while ago and did very well. I bought a
wardrobe and a chest of drawers in Ikea, then I went to Boots and
bought some suppositories. Believe it or not, I managed to put them
all up myself.

Before he went to the great workshop in the sky (... he did like
a big hammer) Hector was never very good at DIY, although he
did try his best. He did woodwork and metalwork classes at school.
Unfortunately, he made a coffee table in metalwork and a poker in
woodwork. The coffee table lasted for years, the wooden poker ... not
quite so long ...

Dear Aunty May

I don't live at home any more but I do miss it. Last time I visited, I suspected that my Dad – who has worked for the Council roads department for 30 years – might be stealing. How can I find out for sure?

Sylvia

Dear Sylvia

Just go back home. I'm sure all the signs will be there.

Aunty M

Dear Aunty May

We are going to decorate our front room. I know that your house is the same as mine, and I wondered if I could ask for your help. How many rolls of wallpaper did you buy for your front room?

Esther

Dear Esther

I'm happy to help. I bought sixteen rolls of wallpaper.

Aunty M

Dear Aunty May

Thank you for your reply. The living room's done now, but I have four rolls of wallpaper left over.

Esther

Dear Esther

That's funny, so had I!

Aunty M

Our homes, friends and families are just so important to us all. My old friend, Bruce is coming over for a visit from Australia next year and I'm so looking forward to seeing him again!

I've known Bruce since I was a young girl, as we were pen pals. Pen pals are what we had before Facebook friends, except they were real people who wrote real letters with pen, ink, paper and stamps. Letters would take weeks to arrive, unlike now when folk go mad if they don't get replies to their messages in a hearbeat.

BRUCE
THE
AUSSIE

Bruce and I wrote to each other for years. He'd tell me all about his didgeridoo and send me pictures of his wallaby. I'd write back and send him pictures of my wee Toot Toot (I always thought that was an unusual name for a hamster).

The first time he came over to visit me, I got all carried away with visions of romance. Sadly, it wasn't to be as he turned out to be shorter and fatter than he was in his photos, with corks swinging everywhere and a voice so high that only dogs could hear him.

I think it's best not to romanticize the past and live firmly in the here and noo. Still, although Bruce and I turned out to be firm friends, if we'd had Facetime way back then, it would have saved me a lot of heartache!

I'm lucky to have so many visitors and my brother, Doogle comes to stay with me a couple of times a year. He doesn't have much hair but he's a mine of information. He just reads and reads and surfs and surfs the interweb all day long. That's why I always say if I don't know something, I just Doogle it.

He stayed for a week last time he was here. It was nice to see him but as he's very messy, all I remember was him trailing a flurry of dirty socks and pants in his wake.

One of the many things I miss about my Hector is that he was so tidy. Since he went to the great launderette in the sky (... he loved washing) it's now up to me to keep everything ship-shape around the house.

DOOGLE MY BRO.

Let me tell you, cleaning up after Doogle was a full time job! He never noticed the mess he was making as his eyes were glued to a screen all the while, his computer connected to the interweb with a dongle. I can tell you that Doogle with a dongle is a nightmare.

Still, I don't think my brother's ever been the same since he met a Thai woman on the interweb. He was so smitten, he hopped on a plane to Bangkok but ended up getting more than he bargained for. He had assumed all along that she was a Lady. Boy, how much more wrong could he have been?

Dear Aunty May

I'm scared to take my tiny Chihuahua out for a walk as she just seems so small and vulnerable. What should I do?

Liz

Dear Liz

I wouldn't worry. Many years ago we had a tiny little Chihuahua that killed a massive Doberman Pinscher stone deid ... it got stuck in its throat.

Aunty M

Since my dear Hector went to the great menagerie in the sky (... he loved a cockatoo) it's just me and Mini May at home now. Still, we're in our own wee routine. I snuggle down on the sofa with a nice cup of cocoa and a hobnob, and she snuggles onto my lap with a nice wee chew and a bonio.

We like to watch TV together and we think we're like those folk on our favourite programme, Gogglebox. Mini May always has something to say about that David Attenborough. She reckons that he should stay away from the Amazon Rainforest and hoof it over to Morningside Park. She says he'll get an eyeful of how wild life can be, especially on a Saturday night when the pubs come out.

Dear Aunty May

Every time I take my wee terrier to the park, she gets pursued by a big overly amorous smelly fluffy white dog. What should I do?

Mr McClusky

Dear Mr McClusky

There's nothing worse than a frisky musky husky. Take your wee terrier out to the park when it's deserted, just after dusky.

Aunty M

Dear Aunty May

I have read that you have a Cockapoo. That's a cross between a Cocker Spaniel and a Poodle, isn't it? Well, I have a Shih Tzu and my friend has a Poodle. We were wondering if we should 'get them together', if you know what I mean?

Ami

Dear Ami

A Shitpoo? Oh no, dear. I don't think so.

Aunty M

IT WASN'T ME

Dear Aunty May

I came down to the kitchen this morning to find Tweety, my budgie lying on the bottom of the cage. I gave her mouth-to-beak resuscitation and managed to revive her. Unfortunately, she had broken her little leg. I thought that was the end of her, but my friend suggested getting a match and using it as a splint. I did that, and she's been fine for over a week now.

Cathy

Dear Cathy

Well done! I'm so pleased you managed to save your wee Tweety. It's amazing how you can become so attached to a little bird. Let me know how she is getting on.

Aunty M

Dear Aunty May

Unfortunately, Tweety has gone. I'm so upset. Everything was fine 'til she dragged her foot along the sandpaper on the bottom of the cage. She lit up like a Christmas tree.

Cathy

Dear Cathy

Sorry to hear that. A little lesson to be learned there.

Aunty M

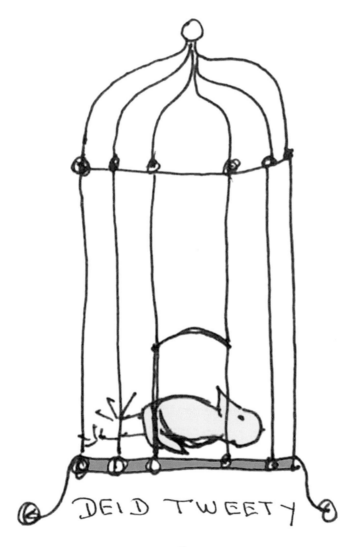

DEID TWEETY

EVERYBODY NEEDS GOOD NEIGHBOURS

Dear Aunty May

My next door neighbour is always complaining about her aches and pains. Although I try to be sympathetic, it does get a bit wearing after a while. Last time I visited her, she just went on and on about her chilblains and her bunions. I think I'm going to stop visiting. Am I being a bad neighbour?

Isobel

Dear Isobel

You're not being a bad neighbour. Some people are born moaners.

I have a friend and she's very old. Last week she phoned and said she had a terrible pain two inches below her left breast. I was genuinely worried.

I thought, 'two inches below her left breast? That's her heart!'

I immediately called the doctor and cried, 'I think my friend's having a heart attack!'

Turns out that two inches below her left breast was her knee. I felt very silly.

Aunty M

Household List:

– Put bin out

– Take bin in

– Set up net trap for Parcel Force delivery man

– Make trip to recycling bin to dispose of
  empty wine bottles

– On second thoughts, make two trips

– Tidy house before cleaner gets here

– Move half my wardrobe from the chair by the
  side of the bed

– Get some Vanish - can't find the other bottle

– Try to find that camouflage jumper

I've lived in the same house for over forty years. That's mainly because I have such lovely neighbours.

There's Nora at Number 57. She's tried every diet under the sun. The last one she was on was the F plan diet, which made her have beans with everything. She had beans on toast, beans and eggs, beans and bacon, beans and chips, beans and beans …

I tell you one thing – now I know what the F stands for! Nora's probably the main cause of climate change.

Then there are Daniel and Guy who live at Number 78. They swore they weren't gay for such a long time – 'we're just good friends' they used to say. Then, all of a sudden they draped the house in bunting and flashing lights, and decided to have a 'Coming Out' fancy dress party. Oh, what a night that was!

Hector, Maggie, and I went dressed as the Village People, and Nora put a piece of string up her bum and went as a balloon. Greig from Number 43 went as Danny La Rue but was a bit too convincing, if you ask me. Sheila from Number 65 covered herself in carrier bags and went as the Lidl mermaid.

George and Sara from Number 62 really pushed the boat out. George wore a Tesco uniform and Sara stuck to his side all night, wearing a paper bag over her head. Hector thought it was hilarious when George said that Sara was his 'Bag for Life'.

Daniel has something to do with Scottish politics, so he invited Nicola Sturgeon along to the party. We couldn't wait to find out whether she'd come in fancy dress or not. She did! She was a great sport, walking in on her knees dressed as a wee schoolboy. Mind, you never see her and Wee Jimmy Krankie in the same room ... funny, that.

Dear Aunty May

I feel so sorry for George my next door neighbour, who is 92. He always wished he had met Elvis Presley.

Mabel

Dear Mabel

92? Ninety-two? NINETY-TWO? Tell George it won't be long now.

Aunty M

Dear Aunty May

I'm very upset about the present my husband bought me for my Christmas. He seemed so pleased with himself when he got me a belt and bag.

Angela

Dear Angela

They seem like perfectly good presents, I don't see why you're unhappy.

Aunty M

Dear Aunty May

The hoover didn't even need a new belt and bag.

Angela

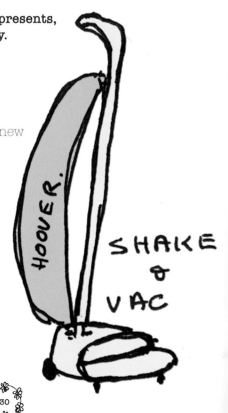

My neighbours in the big house on the corner, Heidi and Hilda, are two lovely ladies. They've lived together for over twenty years. Twenty years, fancy that!

They know that I'm busy during panto season so they often drop off a steak pie, a pot of stovies, or a plate of my favourite mince and tatties. To thank them, I gave them a couple of tickets for the panto.

When I saw them in the audience I shouted, 'Oh look! It's the Ugly Sisters, Aldi and Lidl!' They were laughin', but they wurnae happy.

They're devoted friends, though. Heidi lost her husband 25 years ago (… what a card game that was) and Hilda is a cleaner at the public toilets at Waverley Station. She hates the job, but says it stops her biting her nails

Dear Aunty May

My next door neighbour is a flasher. He's getting old now and his wife has told him to retire. What do you think?

Shona

Dear Shona

I think he should stick it out 'til Christmas.

Aunty M

In the privacy of our own homes, we do all sorts of things we wouldn't want folk to know about, don't we? Why, no-one knows that late at night I like to practice my yodelling in the pantry.

I learned to yodel on one of the many trips I made to Switzerland with my dear departed Hector, long before he went to the great Alpine range in the sky ... he loved a Toblerone.

FOOD, GLORIOUS FOOD

Dear Aunty May

I love fish and seafood, and have tried cooking most types. One of the only types I haven't tried is octopus. What is the best way to cook it?

Helen

Dear Helen

I like to boil octopus in a large pot of salted water. However, I'd suggest that you stick it on top of the stove early in the afternoon. The last one I cooked took three hours because the octopus kept reaching out and switching the gas off.

Aunty M

Dear Aunty May

I've had an extra large pizza delivered every night for a month and ate each one sitting in front of the TV. I've had a ball but have just found out that the local pizzeria has closed down, and now none of my clothes fit. I'm really sad, what should I do?

Rupert

Dear Rupert

No wonder you're sad! You're having a real run of bad luck, what with your pizzeria shutting down and all of your clothes shrinking.

Aunty M

I was food shopping the other day and found myself at the fruit section. Well, I got myself there actually.

Anyhoo, I do love grapes but as I was looking at the whole array on display I started to wonder why they still make grapes with pips in them. They are so annoying. Surely nobody wants to have to spit all those pips into the waste paper bin from their dining table any more.

I know that pip-spitting provided families up and doon the country with hours of endless fun over the years, but now we have Netflix.

SEEDS OR NAE SEEDS. THAT IS THE QUESTION

Shopping List:

– Grapes (seedless)

– Sausages (skinless)

– Bacon (rindless)

– Bread (crustless)

– Milk (fatless)

– Custard (lumpless)

– Carrots (topless)

– Hummus (pointless)

Pointless? Have never understood that TV show.

I love my food. My dear Hector made some wonderful concoctions before he went to the great restaurant in the sky … he loved waitresses. Before we were married, he told me that he loved spotted dick. I nearly dumped him there and then.

After we got married, it wasn't long before he was doing all the cooking. I wasn't very good at it. He loved Chinese food and had been taught how to rustle up a few recipes by his friend, Won Hung Low. His prawn balls were wonderful.

One night when Maggie was coming round for dinner, she asked, 'what is Hector making?'

I replied, 'A spaghetti bollocknaked'.

She said, 'Don't you mean Spaghetti Bolognese?'

I replied, 'I know what I mean!'

He did have some strange ways, did my Hector.

Dear Aunty May

Every time I go into one of these fancy coffee shops, I get all confused and don't know what to order. Whatever happened to ordering just a plain old cup of coffee?

Violet

Dear Violet

Maggie worked in a Starbucks for a while. One of those yuppie types came in and asked for a double shot skinny vanilla decaf frappuccino extra hot with foam and whipped cream, so she punched him ... she doesn't work there anymore.

As for me, I was feeling a wee bit glum the other day. I had heard somewhere that a nice cup of coffee cheers you up, so I found myself in Starbucks. Well, I got myself there actually.

I asked for a Depresso. I don't know why, but they sniggered.

Then they asked me, 'What name do you want on the cup?'

I replied, 'Mine!'

Eejits! I'm no' goin' back.

Aunty M

You know what I miss? Creamola Foam. How I loved popping that little piece of paper when you opened a new can! I liked the lemon flavour the best. The Hendry's lemonade van roared down our street once a week, but Creamola Foam kept me going between their deliveries. Happy days.

Why is everything so complicated now? Whatever happened to Mother's Pride bread? Why do they call a courgette a zucchini? What on earth is a kumquat? Why did they change Jif to Cif? When did Opal Fruits turn into Starburst? Why did they change the Marathon bar into a Snickers? Just as I was getting used to saying, 'gie us a Snickers, pal' in our corner shop, they decide to change it back again ... make up your minds! Och, I'm away for a wee lie doon.

Dear Aunty May

I went to the fruit shop yesterday and asked for 4 pounds of potatoes. The man behind the counter said, 'It's kilos now, dear!'

I said, 'Oh sorry, can I have 4 pounds of kilos please?'

Everybody laughed.

Patricia

Dear Patricia

Don't you worry ma darling, it was probably those eejits in Europe that changed the name. Brexit means that we can go back to calling them potatoes.

Aunty M

KEEPING UP APPEARANCES

Dear Aunty May

I'm 70 years old and have finally decided that it's time to have a boob job. They say that men prefer women with a big bosom. Do you think I should go ahead and have it done?

Beryl

Dear Beryl

I wouldn't bother if I were you. Be happy in your own skin.

My dear departed husband Hector used to say that any more than a handful is a waste. So if I were you, I'd save my money and find a man with tiny hands.

Trump might be your man.

Aunty M

BIGA BOOBIES   SMALL HANDS

Dear Aunty May

I am 72 years old and thinking of getting a face lift. You might think I don't need it (I've enclosed a photo of me in my birthday suit) but I've recently started dating again and have noticed that it's only the very old men that are showing any interest in me. Thing is, I'm after someone younger. What do you think I should do?

Agnes

Dear Agnes

Someone younger? Go get 'em! Mind you, from your photo I would say that although the face lift is up to you, I do think your birthday suit could do with ironing.

I visited my American friend last year who'd recently had some bits stretched up and some 'work' done. When I asked her what the pronounced spot on her chin was, she said it was her belly button.

I decided not to mention her beard.

Aunty M

I've had the same doctor for years. He knows me inside out. The other day, I said to him, 'I think I have Tourette's.'

He asked, 'What makes you think that?'

I said, 'Well, I have this constant ringing in my ears.'

He said, 'No, that is Tinnitus.'

He said, 'Tourette's is when you swear all the time.'

'Oh bugger,' I said, 'I've got that as well.'

Dear Aunty May

There has been a lot of stuff in the press recently about how often you should wash your bra. I only wash mine twice a week.

Gary

Dear Gary

Me too.

Aunty M

I think it's important to be grateful for what Mother Nature blessed us with when it comes to our bodies and our looks. I remember my dear departed Hector started losing his hair not long after we were married.

One day he asked me, 'Do you think I should A) get a wig or B) ... ?'

Well, I'd shouted 'B' before he'd even had time to finish his question!

I quickly told him that I found bald men sexy. I didn't, but it made him feel better.

Hector's now gone to the great barber's shop in the sky ... he loved a good comb-over. Towards the end, mind you, he was as bald as a coot. What is a coot? And just how bald is it?

Dear Aunty May

I have noticed that my teeth are very yellow, and people comment on them all the time. What can you suggest?

Craig

Dear Craig

A brown tie.

Aunty M

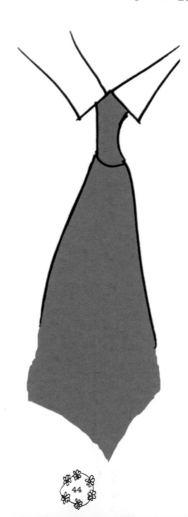

Dear Aunty May

An expert recently suggested to me that I should have a regular enema to make me feel light and fresh and free. I hate it, what should I do?

Barry

Dear Barry

Light and fresh and free? My Hector told me that during the war he was given three enemas in a row one day. He'd had enough and locked himself in the loo.

When the nurse came looking for him and knocked on the door he shouted, 'Halt! Don't come any closer! Friend or Enema?'

Aunty M

Dear Aunty May

Someone once told me that the cure for baldness is to smear cow dung over your head. What do you think?

Samuel

Dear Samuel

I think that if you smear cow dung over your head, no-one will come near enough to notice.

Aunty M

COO POO

Here's a wee tip for all you men out there. A wig looks like a wig. Sorry to be so blunt, but it's true. There are a few men who think that their wig doesn't look like a wig. Trust me, it looks like a wig.

If Elton, Sinatra and Brucie, with all their money and their tip-top hairdressers couldn't get it right, chances are you're not going to get it right either. No matter how much time you spend grooming your thatch, no matter how good you think it looks, it's going to look like a wig.

Sorry, am I repeating myself? Well, I tend to do that on matters of importance.

Wigs! Fail! End of!

HECTOR'S WIGGY

GETTING DOWN WITH THE KIDS

Dear Aunty May

My children send messages to me using all sorts of silly abbreviations like OMG and LOL. After suffering a mild panic attack, I found out that CNT means Can't Talk Now. It's too much for me. I just don't understand it all. Can you suggest what I should do?

Sarah

Dear Sarah

I know what you mean. The other day, I got a text from my minister letting me know that we raised over £3000 for the church roof restoration fund at the summer fete.

I was so excited I texted back 'WTF!'

The minister seemed very annoyed yet all I said was, 'Wow That's Fantastic!'

Hmmm, maybe I'm not the one to help you with this issue of yours.

SCHA – Sorry Can't Help Anymore.

Aunty M

I'm a big fan of sochul medya and got a friend request on Facebook the other day from someone I was at school with. He said he had been living in Italy since he was a wee boy and had always remembered me. He said we had once kissed behind the toilets and asked if I remembered. He sent me a photo of himself. I must say, I don't remember kissing anyone who was bald with a beard.

My friends say that I should start something called a Minstagram page. Apparently, it's where you post pictures of what you eat and tell everyone how wonderful your life is. I doubt that a picture of egg and chips is going to convince anyone that my life is wonderful, but you never know.

Oh, sorry! Maggie has just told me it's called Instagram and if enough people like you, you can become something called an 'influencer'. She told me that's someone who gets paid for posting photos of products they use which will influence other folk to buy them. Maybe I should give it a go. Brace yourself, Instagrammers for some revealing photos of me sporting my Tena Ladies! Now, that would put you off your egg and chips.

My Wee Allan is on Instagram so I joined up and followed him. Well, I say 'followed' but really, I just clicked on a button.

He told me to start 'following' people I knew and before I knew it, I'd started following the back row of the Zumba class, half the male tenors in the choir and most of the origami group.

I needed a wee lie down in a darkened room after being bombarded with their selfies taken from all angles in varying states of undress and inebriation.

Who knew those tenors were so wild? Who knew you could do so much with a piece of paper folded into the shape of a cactus? Botanical week at the origami club will never be the same again.

There are simply some things you shouldn't know about other people's lives. Maybe I should write to myself and get some advice.

Dear Aunty May

My son, who is 6 years old, just hates school. He cries every morning and says he doesn't want to go. I have to drag him there and leave him crying at the gates. It's breaking my heart. Do you think he will grow out of it?

Cheryl

Dear Cheryl

Don't worry, I'm sure he'll grow out of it. I remember that years ago Moira, a friend of mine, had the same problem. Her Johnny got into a terrible state every morning, and cried and cried his eyes out.

He would say, 'I don't want to go to school, I don't want to go, everybody hates me!'

She would very calmly sit him down and say, 'Darling, you have to go – you're the Head Master.'

Aunty M

Writing about young people always takes me back to the old days. I remember when I'd take my Wee Allan out shopping with me. We'd go out for tea and cake, and I'd always buy him some clothes. I so looked forward to those times we spent together.

It was so funny when he'd say, 'Aunty May, I need a wee wee!' I'd take him to the kerb and he'd do it in the gutter with all the cars going by. He hated that. Mind you … he was 18.

Dear Aunty May

My son, who is 12 years old, has been sent home from school three times now for weeing in the swimming pool. I have taken away his phone and threatened him with no games if he doesn't stop. Am I doing the right thing?

Susanna

Dear Susanna

I think you're being a bit harsh on him. We all know that kids wee in the swimming pool, don't we?

Aunty M

Dear Aunty May

Thank you for your answer, but I should have told you that he's doing it from the high diving board.

Susanna

Dear Susanna

Ahhhh!

Aunty M

Over the years, I've received many letters from both parents and children. I recall that one teenage girl wrote to say that her Mum had lied to her a lot during childhood. Now the girl felt like she couldn't trust her anymore. She said that her mother had told her there was a tooth fairy and that Santa Claus was real.

I answered that she shouldn't blame her mother as these are just little white lies which are told to help you through childhood.

I told her that my own Mum would say to me, 'I'll count and see how long it takes you to run upstairs and get my jacket!'

She would start counting ... 1, 2, 3 ... I'd run upstairs, race back down and there she'd be, still counting ... 24, 25 26 ...

'Well done!' she'd say, 'that was quicker than last time!'

I told the girl that it took me twenty years to find out that as soon as I went out of the room, my Mum would stop counting, lie back and put her feet up. As soon as she heard me coming back, she'd start counting again.

I can't blame my Mum as this was just one of the little white lies she told me to help her through my childhood.

Dear Aunty May

I was telling my son that we used to play a game where we knocked on someone's door, then ran away before they could answer. I think it was called Knock Knock Ginger. Do you have any idea what it's called now?

Karen

Dear Karen

Parcel Force.

Aunty M

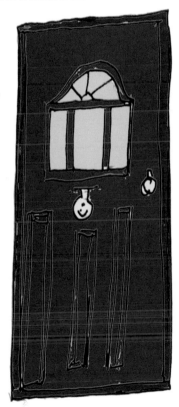

← BIG KNOCKER.

HEALTH AND HAPPINESS

Dear Aunty May

As a man of 65, I like to keep fit and make sure my health is 100%.

Recently I went for one of my regular check-ups. Everything was fine 'til I felt a finger up my bottom. Well, this had never happened before. Imagine my shock! I'm not sure I want to go back next year. What do you suggest?

Billy

Dear Billy

You should find yourself a new dentist.

Aunty M

Dear Aunty May

My husband has got terrible piles. He has tried everything, but nothing seems to work. Can you suggest anything?

Sheena

Dear Sheena

My Hector had terrible hemorrhoids for years, before he went to the warm soothing bath in the sky ... he loved a rubber duck.

A friend told him to use a tea bag to shrink them. When he was next at the doctor, he pulled down his pants and the tea bag burst. There were tea leaves everywhere!

'What do you think, doctor?' asked Hector.

The doctor replied, 'I think you're going on a long journey and will meet a tall dark stranger.'

Aunty M

My best friend Maggie has recently been in hospital. When she was in there she had it all taken away – tables, chairs, wardrobes, the lot! Before her operation, she was embarrassed because she had to be shaved in a very particular place. She told me that it was such a long time since she shaved down there, it was like a forest.

Apparently, a young trainee nurse was assigned to do the job. Her embarrassment wasn't helped when she'd heard him mutter, 'It's like I'm in I'm A Celebrity Get Me Out of Here and I'm doing my first bush tucker trial!'

Dear Aunty May

I am 76 and have had chest pains for some time now. My doctor says I have acute angina. Is this bad?

Angie

Dear Angie

No, it's not bad and at your age I'd take any compliment I could get.

Aunty M

I have to say that getting old is no fun. Inside, I feel all of 22 but as much as I hate to admit it, my body gives me wee signs that I'm aging now and then.

All right, my body gives me wee signs a lot of the time.

Okay, my body gives me signs all the time and they're not that wee … that little dribble when I laugh … I can't sleep past 8 o'clock in the morning … I can't stay awake past 9 o'clock at night … the music is too loud … the TV is too quiet … I can never find my glasses, even though they're on a chain around my neck … I have a cupboard full of plastic bags with plastic bags inside them … and I go around the house switching lights off muttering about the electricity bill. No, it's nae fun.

Still, accepting your own mortality is an important step in life. It gets me thinking about my Hector, just before he went to the great chapati in the sky … he loved an Indian.

He gave me a beautiful funeral plot overlooking Edinburgh Castle for my birthday – so thoughtful. When my next birthday came around, I asked him, 'What are you getting me this year?'

He said, 'Nothing! You didn't use the present I got you last year!'

He was such a kidder.

Dear Aunty May

I have a lot of wind at the moment. What should I get for it?

Tracy

Dear Tracy

A kite.

Aunty M

Dear Aunty May

I went to the chemist's to buy some hair removing cream as my lovely wee Schnauzer has an unsightly bit of hair on his head, between his ears. When the chemist gave me the cream he said, 'Remember when you rub it under your arms, just hold them up 'til they dry.' I replied that it wasn't for under my arms, it was for my Schnauzer.

Ethel

Dear Ethel

I'm going to stop you right there. I suspect he also told you not to ride your bike for a week.

Aunty M

Dear Aunty May

I left my husband, I left my job, and I have started to put on weight. I need to look my best. What diet do you suggest I try?

Mabel

Dear Mabel

You've obviously had a lot on your plate!

I have always liked the Dr Atkins diet. You don't eat any carbs or any sugar for a week, then you go to the chemist and he gives you little box of sticks. When you get up in the morning, you wee on the stick. If it turns purple, it means you've lost some weight but if your shoes turn green, it means you've missed the stick.

Aunty M

Dear Aunty May

I am an opera singer and everyone tells me I look like Placido Domingo. I'm thinking of performing as a lookalike tribute act, 'The One Tenor' but I suffer from terrible stage fright. Do you have any suggestions?

Antonio

Dear Antonio

Pop a wee sugar pill, imagine it's a wee Beta blocker and call yourself Placebo Domingo.

Aunty M

P.S. Don't undersell yourself. I'm sure you'll get more than a tenor.

I went out and bought some nice new lycra. I looked like the Michelin Man! Still, I persevered and went to a few classes. The thing was, every day after I finished my class I was starving, so I went to a café and had coffee and cake. By the end of the month, I'd put on half a stone.

That was end of that.

Dear Aunty May

I have had diah ... direa ... dihre ... the runs for a couple of weeks now. Can you suggest any home remedies that might help?

John

Dear John

I'll tell you a wee secret. When I had dia ... dihre ... diahre ... the runs I took two teaspoons of Bisto every morning.

It doesn't cure it but it does thicken it.

Aunty M

Dear Aunty May

I have had very bad piles for some time now. I've tried all the different creams but they don't work. I went to the doctor and he gave me these things called suppositories. I've swallowed five of them but there's still no change. For all the good they've done me, I might as well have stuck them up my bum.

Craig

Dear Craig

You may be onto something. Just saying.

Aunty M

GETTING AWAY FROM IT ALL

Dear Aunty May

I'm 72 years old and have decided to go on a cruise on my own. I've never cruised before and I've no idea what to expect but I know you've been on cruises many times with your Wee Allan. What is it like? Is there any chance of me meeting a man?

Mabel

Dear Mabel

Many people ask me what cruising is like and I always reply with a question: 'do you like hotels?'

'Well, it's just like a hotel,' I say, 'except that it can sink.' I like to put people's minds at rest.

As far as romance is concerned, don't hold your breath. From what I've seen, the single men on cruises are aged anywhere between 70 and deid.

I once sat next to an old gentleman at sea and after a little tipple, I thought I'd make a little light-hearted advance. I leaned over and asked him, 'Would you like super sex?'

He turned round to me slowly and answered, 'If it's all the same to you, I'd rather have the soup.'

Aunty M

Dear Aunty May

My husband and I are going on a weekend break to Venice
for our anniversary. I've heard that the restaurants there rip
you off by charging silly prices. Have you ever been?

Sarah

Dear Sarah

**Yes, I went to Venice with my friend, Maggie last year and
very nice it was too. I'd advise you to play it clever when
you're in restaurants there. After having a cup of coffee in
St Mark's Square, a waiter presented Maggie and I with
a bill of 45 Euros.**

I said, 'That's ridiculous, young man! Why is it so expensive?'

**'Well,' he replied, 'the band was playing so that is what you
are paying for.'**

I replied, 'But we didn't listen to the band.'

**'Well it was there if you wanted it,' he said, 'and there was
a biscuit on your plate.'**

'We didn't eat the biscuit,' I replied.

'It was there if you wanted it,' he said.

I said, 'Okay, in that case you owe us 100 Euros.'

He asked, 'Why?'

I said, 'That's for having sex with Maggie.'

He said, 'Whoa, I didn't have sex with her!'

I said, 'Yes, but it was there if you wanted it.'

That shut him up! He presented us with a bill for 8 Euros, and we paid up and left.

Aunty M

JUST ONE CORNETTO (€40.)

I always say that a change is as good as a rest so a wee while ago, I hopped down to London to spend time with my Wee Allan and recharge my batteries.

As a surprise, he took me to The O2 to see that Huge Jackman from the films. Who knew that Huge could sing and dance and do all sorts of things with his clothes on? One of the people on stage even had a massive didgeridoo. The surprises just kept on coming!

During one sad ballad, the arena was plunged into darkness and Huge asked everyone to wave their phones in the air with their torches on. What a sight it was, to see thousands of lights shining around the arena! My old Nokia didn't have a light on it. I didn't want to be left out so I waved it anyhoo.

It reminded me of the time all these years ago, when I saw Calum Kennedy play live at the Dockers Club. That night, he'd asked everyone to fire up their lighters and hold them above their heads. It didn't end well. The sprinklers went off. I would have loved to have seen someone like Calum play The O2.

Happy days

Dear Aunty May

My husband wants to take me on a skiing holiday to
Switzerland. I'm scared in case I break my leg. Do you
think I should go?

Tracy

Dear Tracy

**My Hector took me skiing in Switzerland many years ago,
before he went to the great cuckoo clock in the sky ... he
loved an Alpine horn.**

**I remember that I bought him a lovely pair of leather
Lederhosen but he said they were too rough and got a bad
case of chafing.**

**I think you should give it a try
– the skiing, not the Lederhosen.**

Aunty M

Dear Aunty May

My daughter and son-in-law are taking me to Spain for a summer holiday. I have never been abroad and since I don't know any Spanish words, I'm worried about how I'm going to communicate. Can you help me?

Mavis

Dear Mavis

Here are a couple of phrases I always find useful when I'm in Spain:

el bogo del senorita – the ladies toilet

uno mugo del plonko – one glass of wine

Otherwise, you can manage to get by using Spanglish. It's quite easy, you just make it up as you go along. For example:

How much-o is el ticket for el bus-o tae Torremolinos?

Where-o is el parking for el sandy beach-o?

You see? It's a piece of cake-o!

Have fun!

Aunty M

SOMBRERO 'O'

Dear Aunty May,

I was telling a friend that I was going on holiday next year to Majorca. He said in Spain it's not pronounced Majorca it's Mayorca - you don't say the 'J' you say 'y'.

He asked me, 'When are you going?'

I replied, 'The last week in Yune and first week in Yuly.'

At that time of year, what should I wear to travel?

Senga

Dear Senga

I always think you should feel comfortable when you're travelling, so I suggest you just wear a pair of yeans and a yumper.

Aunty M

YEANS   YUMPER.

Dear Aunty May

My husband wants to take me on a cruise for the first time, from Southampton to Madeira. However, the prospect of being away at sea scares me. I looked at the map and it's such a long way! I just can't understand how the captain will be able to find Madeira in such a vast expanse of water. You've cruised a lot, can you help?

Tracy

Dear Tracy

Please don't worry, the captain will find it – it's a piece of cake.

Aunty M

I do love to travel with my friend Maggie. The other week, we went to Amsterdam for a wee break. What a beautiful place! It has lots of canals and lovely restaurants.

We went into a wee café where a nice man asked us if we would like to try his special brownies. Well, Maggie and I are very partial to a wee chocolate brownie or two but oh, these were spectacular! We enjoyed them so much that we took a couple back to the hotel to eat before bedtime.

That night we went to a play. The two of us laughed our heads off which was strange it was all in Hollandish, so we didn't understand a word, and loads of the characters died. Still, we had a high old time to ourselves ... funny, that.

I didn't care that I'd forgotten to wear my Tena Ladies, and really didn't care when members of the audience started tut-tutting, pointing at the seepage and muttering things about 'the bloody British'. Maggie and I were having a ball!

After the play finished, we went back to the hotel, had tea and polished off the brownies we'd bought earlier. We snuggled down in our pyjamas and watched Titanic. Oh, how we laughed!

Holiday Packing

- Pandrops

- Rainmate

- Galoshes

- Maggie's blue umbrella

- Lavender eye mask

- 4711

- Poncho

- Any book by Jackie Collins

- A felt tip pen to scribble oot anything rude written by Jackie Collins

Oops, forgot:

- Passport

- Tickets

- Money

Dear Aunty May

I'm 68 years old and am thinking of going to a nudist camp for my summer holidays for the first time. I'm quite a shy person and am worried that I won't know what to say to a woman when we first meet. What do you suggest?

Simon

Dear Simon

Just talk about the first thing that pops up.

Aunty M

LOVE AND MARRIAGE

Dear Aunty May

I'm 82 and my fiancé is 84. We're getting married in a couple of months' time and everyone's asking us about wedding presents. I think the most sensible thing is to register a wedding list somewhere. Do you have any suggestions?

Audrey

Dear Audrey

Boots.

Aunty M

OVER 80'S WEDDING PRESENTS

I receive a lot of letters from people of all ages who aren't sure about whether or not to accept marriage proposals. What I always tell them is, 'If you're not sure, don't do it!'

If you find the other person's habits slightly irritating now, they'll send you so far round the twist in five, ten or twenty years' time that you'll never find your way back!

So ask yourself questions like: does he make a noise when he drinks his tea? Does she take more than two hours to get ready before you go out? Does he fall asleep on the sofa holding the remote control, and when you try to take it from him to change the channel, he suddenly wakes up and says, 'I was watching that'? Does she hog the whole duvet and roll herself up tight, like a Gregg's sausage roll? Does he break wind and pull the covers over your head? Urrrgh. Think on!

Dear Aunty May

I'm so confused about all this gender fluidity thing everyone's talking about. Recently, I caught my husband trying on one of my frocks. He said he just wanted to know what it felt like to feel the cotton next to his skin. Should I be worried that he might be a transvestite?

Bella

Dear Bella

I wouldn't be worried. If your husband is a transvestite, at worst you'll double your wardrobe. Remember – first up in the morning gets the sling backs!

Aunty M

I receive a lot of letters from couples who seem to be jealous of each other. That can ruin a relationship. I was never jealous of Hector but he had an annoying habit of chatting to the weather girl on TV. I wasn't jealous but it was very silly.

I remember he had a fancy for Lucy, one of the weather girls. When it was time for the forecast, he'd shout at the TV, 'Hello Lucy!' or 'Oh, Lucy you're looking lovely today!' or 'Good night, Lucy!'

I just ignored him.

He'd been doing this for months, then one night as he was lying on the couch he said, 'Darling, could you make me a cup of tea?'

I replied, 'Darling, why don't you ask Lucy to make it?'

He never shouted at the TV again.

Dear Aunty May

My lazy husband drives me mad. He never flushes the toilet. I'm forever telling him off, but he just won't do it.

Tina

Dear Tina

Well, as my dear departed husband Hector used to say, before he went to the great bookies in the sky (... he loved horse racing), 'If it's yellow let it mellow, if it's brown flush it down.'

Aunty M

Dear Aunty May

I'm embarrassed to tell you this, but I'm getting married in a couple of weeks' time and I've never had sex with a girl because my thingy is very small. I'm worried about the wedding night.

Tony

Dear Tiny ... sorry ... Tony

Please don't worry, on the wedding night your thingy will be twice the size and there will be two of you looking for it.

Aunty M

Dear Aunty May

When we went on holiday last year, my husband refused to put sunscreen on. As a result, his legs got burnt so badly that he couldn't sleep and it ruined our holiday.

I've told him that if he doesn't start using sunscreen, I'll never go away with him again. Am I right?

Senga

Dear Senga

Well, it's hard to teach an old dog new tricks and you don't really want to miss out on your holidays, do you?

My advice is to go to your doctor and get some Viagra. If your husband's legs get sunburnt again give him a little blue pill. It won't help the sunburn, but it will keep the sheets off his legs.

Sleep tight.

Aunty M

ON THE
BEACH
(FORGOT TO
SHAVE)

GLADIATOR
SANDALS

I knew from the moment I looked into my dear departed Hector's eye
(he only had the one, he lost the other when he crashed his tandem)
that he was the one for me. He was so generous and was always
thinking of me.

I remember the time we were watching the film 'Gladiator' together,
just before he went to the great Colosseum in the sky ... he loved a
toga. We were transfixed by the scene where Maximus fell to the
ground in a pool of blood and guts.

As I gasped in horror, Hector took me in his arms and said, 'May,
do you see the sandals Maximus is wearing?'

'Oh yes,' I replied, 'I do.'

'Well,' he said, 'I'd like to see you in a pair like that in the summer.'
Oh, he loved shoes.

Dear Aunty May

My husband, who has two wooden legs, set the house on fire by dropping a lit cigarette on the living room floor. He had a lucky escape but the house and his legs were burnt to the ground. Do you think the insurance will pay out?

Celia

Dear Celia

I think they will pay for the house but I'm afraid your husband doesn't have a leg to stand on.

Aunty M

Dear Aunty May

My husband comes home from the pub drunk every night, takes off all his clothes, and stands naked in front of the bedroom window. How can I stop him?

Cathy

Dear Cathy

Just say to him, 'come back from the window or the neighbours will think I only married you for your money!'

Aunty M

Dear Aunty May

My husband gets up at least three times a night to go
to the loo for a wee. It wakes me up and I can't get back
to sleep. I've suggested separate bedrooms but he says
he can't sleep without me next to him. What should I do?

Marge

Dear Marge

**I had the same problem with my husband, Hector, so I bought
him some Tena Ladies. Every night he put them on (he needed
two) and just let it go whenever he wanted. We both slept like
babies and had the added joy of
waking up to a rainbow over
the bed in the morning.**

Aunty M

**P.S. There is a website that might help you.
It's www.forward slash forward slash forward slash**

I know that we women say we want equality, but I do appreciate a bit of thoughtfulness like having the door opened for me, or having someone walk on the outside of the pavement so I don't get splashed by a horse, or someone putting the toilet seat down after they've been into the wee small room.

My Hector, before he went to the great wool shop in the sky (... he loved knitting) didn't just make sure that he put the toilet seat down, he knitted a toilet seat cover for me with my name on it.

Now, that's not just gentlemanly behaviour, that's love.

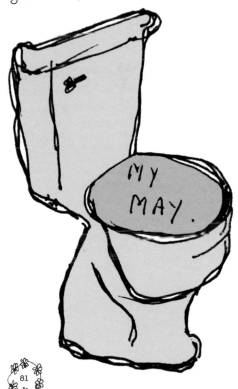

Dear Aunty May

I was making a roast dinner one Sunday when my husband said, 'I'll just nip out to get some broccoli' but he never came back. It's been five years now and I keep on wondering if I did anything wrong. What would you have done?

Catherine

Dear Catherine

I'd have opened a tin of peas.

Aunty M

Many people have written to me about love and marriage over the years, although the two don't necessarily go together. At the start it's all lovey-dovey, but it often goes downhill from there. By the time two kids, a mortgage and a dug come along, folk are barely on speaking terms. Have you ever sat in a restaurant and watched couples staring at each other, not saying a word?

I was so lucky with my dear Hector. We always had something to talk about, mainly because he had so many interests. We spent many a happy hour discussing ways to treat the chafing from his leather Lederhosen. Oh, how I miss spreading that cream on his thighs!

Dear Aunty May

My dear husband, John has passed away. We were happily married for 42 years. He worked in the cotton industry for most of his life and was a wonderful man. Have you any suggestions as to what we could put on his gravestone?

Alice

Dear Alice

I am so sorry to hear about your husband. I know all too well how hard this time of life must be for you.

I think it would be nice to have a simple little message engraved – something like: 'Here lies my dear husband, John. Gone, but not for cotton'.

Aunty M

THE DATING GAME

Dear Aunty May

I was recently at a ceilidh where a man who was wearing full Highland dress singled me out for a lot of attention. He cut a dash in his kilt and kept asking me up to dance. Then, at the end of the night he asked me if I wanted to go back to his room for a wee dram.

I do like a man in a kilt, but being a lady I said 'No, certainly not.'

He replied, 'Come on, you've got a glint in your eye.'

I was shocked and didn't know what to say. What would you have said?

Betty

Dear Betty

I would have said, 'I might have a glint in my eye but you've got a tilt in your kilt. I'm no' comin'!'

Aunty M

Dear Aunty May

I've been registered on an internet dating site for six years now. All I do is scroll endlessly through women's profiles, sometimes for hours on end – it's something I find exciting. The profile of a lovely woman called Victoria keeps catching my eye, but I've never had the nerve to contact her. Do you think internet dating is for me?

Fergus

Dear Fergus

What you're doing is a bit like looking in a baker's window and never buying a cake. It's time to get in there and get yer mooth into a bit of Victoria (sponge).

See what I did there?

Aunty M

I got lonely after my Hector left me for the big distillery in the sky (... he loved his whisky) but I learned how to be content in my own company. I would often look back and smile when I dreamed of days gone by, and remembered stories like the one about poor Hector's Grandad, who tragically drowned in a vat of whisky. Mind you, he did get out three times to pee.

Still, as the years passed, I started to think that I might like some company, especially when I found myself alone on cruise ships time and again. I would find myself standing on deck, looking far out to sea, trying to send a wish-you-were-here text to Maggie (she keeps her feet on land, the ol' Seasick Sadie) and failing because there's no phone signal at sea.

One of the origami girls mentioned that there was an online dating site that I might want to try which caters for the finer needs of ladies and gentlemen of a certain maturity. It's called Grab-a-Granny.

After swiping left, right, up, and down for weeks, I finally went on a few dates and I soon found out that geriatric dating isn't for sissies. You need to get your Big Girl Pants on – the ones with the reinforced gusset!

One 'gentleman' asked me, over a plate of oysters, whether I was any good at ironing. Another one, over a chocolate gateau, asked me if I'd ever fancied pole dancing. A third one, over a bottle of Buckfast, told me that he liked a flumph every night. I told him that he looked as if one flumph a year would do him in, and that he should just go and flumph off – and when he gets there, he should flumph off some more!

Dear Aunty May

Do you think there's any chance of me meeting a nice man in my local supermarket?

Shirley

Dear Shirley

The supermarket is a perfect place to meet members of the opposite sex as it lets you have a wee peek into their lifestyle. Your mission, should you choose to accept it, is to stage a three pronged attack.

First, trawl up and down the aisles looking for someone who's carrying a basket, instead of pushing a huge family-sized trolley.

Second, home in on someone whose basket contains luxury items such as champagne, smoked salmon, and caviar.

Third, if their basket contains vegan sausage rolls, Blue Nun, and Izal shiny toilet rolls ... avoid them like the plague.

Aunty M

P.S. Dear vegans, nae offence.

Dear Aunty May

I went out on a fabulous first date with a lovely man the other week. We held hands, we walked in the park, and he carved our initials into a tree. Don't you think that's romantic?

Hannah

Dear Hannah

Run. For. Your. Life. Didn't you think it strange that he brought a knife on a first date?

Aunty M

After experimenting with online dating, I was ready to throw in the towel, hang up my dancing shoes and resign myself to flumph-free singledom. But then I met Duncan, a very nice man who worked behind the scenes at the theatre.

One night, as he was coming up the back passage, he took a little selfie with me and started chatting. The next day we went out for afternoon tea and scones, and gossiped away about all things theatrical.

He was no Hector, but I thought he'd do ... for noo.

Dear Aunty May

I recently met a man who described himself in his internet dating profile as 'one of the richest men in the world'. He was just lovely, but he arrived on a skateboard and drank tap water all night. Do you think there's a chance he might not be altogether truthful?

Gully

Dear Gully

You have to be very careful when reading internet dating profiles. They contain hidden meanings. For instance:

'adventurous' – slept with everyone

'average looking' – a face only a mother could love

'fun' – annoying

'crazy' – really annoying

'open minded' – desperate

'needs soul mate' – scary stalker

Look back over his profile for anything you might have missed.

Aunty M

Dear Aunty May

You're right. I didn't notice that he'd described himself as 'one of the richest men in the world inside'.

Gully

Dear Gully

He's a tree hugger. Aw, that's nice. Good luck to you both.

Aunty M

The thing about sochul medya is that you can find out all sorts of information about people. After my Wee Allan Instagrammed me up, I decided to follow Duncan and I don't mind telling you that I was not a little shocked at what I found. Turns out he'd been taking hundreds of selfies up the back passage with women of all ages and sizes.

Although I'm not sure if they all went on to be taken out for scones of an afternoon, I was not going to heng aboot to find oot! So I called him up and finished it then and there.

Of course, he started to protest but I just told him, 'talk to the hand, because the face ain't listenin! Uh-huh, oh yeah, girl-friend!' (I have no idea what any of this means.)

Dear Aunty May

My boyfriend, who's told me that he wants to marry me, recently invited me to his home for Sunday lunch. Immediately, I could tell that his mother didn't like me. As if that wasn't bad enough, the family dog sank its teeth into my leg and wouldn't let go. What do you think I should do?

Sara

Dear Sara

It's time to move on. A bad tempered dog will eventually let go. A grumpy mother-in-law never will.

Aunty M

Kissing a lot of frogs is one thing but no' finding a Prince anywhere near the muddy pond is quite another. Still, when my friend introduced me to Kurt, I decided to look out my BGP's (Big Girl Pants) again.

Kurt was visiting Scotland, on holiday from LA in the US of A. He took me to the Edinburgh Tattoo because he said he just loved men in skirts (how lucky was I?). He'd been married four times but I assumed that was just because he liked wedding cake. Certainly, he was a very big chap and oh, he did tell some stories.

He told me that he'd once gone out with twins.

'Wasn't it difficult to tell them apart?' I asked.

'No,' he said, 'Jessica painted her nails purple and George had a much deeper voice.'

His little joke did make me laugh. I think it wus a joke.

Dear Aunty May

I've just started going out with a butcher and he told me that you put your finger up a turkey's bum to find out if it's from Norfolk. He says that's where the best turkeys come from. Have you ever heard of that?

Stella

Dear Stella

I've never heard of it, but be careful if he ever asks you where you are from ... just saying.

Aunty M

Kurt ended up proposing to me, even though we'd only been out on three dates. The man must really have loved wedding cake.

The thing is, I just couldn't leave Scotland and go to LA. I'd miss my Wee Allan and I'd miss the panto. When I refused Kurt's proposal, as gently as I could, straight away he asked me for a flumph. Just like that! All he was after was a muckle great bit of cake and a good flumphing. For flumph's sake! Men!

Still, it didn't put me right off. Hope springs eternal!

My next door neighbour, Senga, asked me to go to a speed dating night in Leith the other week. I wasn't that keen but I went along to humour her. I didn't really know what to expect. It didn't go well.

The first man who sat down in front of me said, 'I was hoping for someone younger!' I answered, 'I was hoping for someone with hair!'

That was the end of that.

Dear Aunty May

Several months ago, I took your advice and tried some Botox. Lo and behold, I got a new lease of life and started dating the paper boy. Don't be too worried, he's a 65 year old retiree, delivering papers as a wee side job. Still, I like to call him my paper boy. Thank you for your great advice.

Agnes

Dear Agnes

Very glad to have helped. Now you have your Daily Male delivered (see what I did there?). Enjoy your new life, and your new face.

Aunty M

ALL THINGS CHRISTMAS

Dear Aunty May

My 14 year old son has been very naughty all year long, and was finally expelled from school for smoking. He says he has his eye on a bike for Christmas, what should I say?

Daisy

Dear Daisy

Just you tell him, 'you'd better keep your eye on it 'cos you'll never get your arse on it!'

Aunty M

Dear Aunty May

Our naughty 15 year old son swears all the time. We've told him if he doesn't stop, he won't get a pony for Christmas.

Andy

Dear Andy

Just get a bag of manure and put it under the Christmas tree. When he asks what it is, just answer, 'it was a pony, but it's gone and f***ed off!'

Aunty M

Dear Aunty May

Every Christmas for the last ten years I've gone to visit my son in Australia. As a result, I've always missed your pantomime. Everyone says it's great, and one year I hope to see it!

Claire

Dear Claire

I will talk to our producers and see if we can change the dates to July. Let me know if that suits you.

Aunty M

Dear Aunty May

I recently saw Andy Gray in a show and he was wearing a kilt. Does he wear anything under his kilt?

Caroline

Dear Sweet Caroline

I have asked him and he told me that nothing is worn. It's all in good working order.

Aunty M

Dear Aunty May

I think it's terrible that you make jokes about Grant Stott's acting and singing. I think he's very talented and personally speaking, I only go to the panto to see him.

Lexi Stott

Dear Lexi

I'm so sorry. I will never do another joke at his expense again.

Aunty M

P.S. He's a rotten DJ as well.

Dear Aunty May

I find Andy Gray very sexy. I love his jowls and his little fat hairy legs. Please tell him that if he is looking for a partner, he can call me anytime he wants.

Arthur

(phone number supplied)

Dear Arthur

You have strange taste but I will pass your number on to Andy.

Aunty M

Dear Aunty May

My husband bought me a sexy see-through nightie for my Christmas. I don't see the point of it as you can see my vest through it.

Claire

Dear Claire

As long as it's not a string vest, it will still look sexy.

Aunty M

Dear Aunty May

Everyone always talks and sings about Rudolf the Red-Nosed Reindeer. Why are none of the others ever mentioned?

Billy

Dear Billy

The only other reindeer I know is Brian the Brown-Nosed Reindeer. He was the one behind Rudolf but couldn't stop as quick as him.

Aunty M

Dear Aunty May

As soon as it gets near Christmas, my next door neighbour struts up and down our street dressed in a big red wig, a shiny green satin frock, a pair of bright striped stockings, sporting a face full of make-up and draped from head to toe in twinkling multi-coloured lights. She says she's the best pantomime dame in the whole wide world. Is she?

Holly

Dear Holly

Oh no, she isn't!

Aunty M

Dear Aunty May

Oh yes, she says she is!

Holly

Dear Holly

Oh no, she isn't! Now, that's quite enough, dear.

Aunty M

THE RANDOMNESS OF LIFE

I was watching that show Room 101 the other night and wondered what I would put into it if I was on it.

First off, I'd put in people (usually men) who use cloth hankies. You see them bringing out these disgusting hankies that have been used a dozen times, all stuck together and then they blow their noses and look at it! Straight into Room 101 they'd go!

Next, I'd get rid of poets who write poetry that doesn't rhyme. It's not a poem if it doesn't rhyme and that is all there is to it. I mean, look at this:

I went out one day with a policeman
Who invited me straight out to luncheon
I knew it wouldn't last and I was aghast
When I saw the size of his truncheon.

Now that's a poem!

Mind you, there are so many TV shows that drive me mad! Take Border Patrol, for instance. Yes, go on – take it! You watch it for 45 minutes whilst some poor lady is taken aside, strip searched and her bag gone through with a fine tooth comb. They look high, low, and every which where 'til they eventually find a bag of dried mushrooms. It's just not right.

Oh, and don't get me started on Grand Designs! I like to watch the first 5 minutes, whilst they show us around the original dump, then I tune back in for the last 10 minutes to see the magnificent house they've ended up with. It only needs to be a 15 minute show.

Just out of left field (where is this 'left field' they talk of?) here are a few little tips for you:

Never underestimate a fart.

Fool proof diet: eat less.

Never eat yellow snow.

Don't lick the bowl - flush it like everyone else.

See? With age comes wisdom.

WHEN ALL'S SAID AND DONE

So here we are, almost at the end of my first book. How exciting!
I might win the Booker prize. What do you win anyhoo? A book?
Maybe that Richard and Judy might even put my book into their
fancy Book Club. Mind you, I always feel so sorry for Judy. I think
that Richard's such an eejit!

I must say that I've really enjoyed leafing through my favourite
letters and putting some of my musings down on the page. My
faithful old typewriter has done me well this past year. Hector
would've been proud, but I'm sure he's looking down on me noo
from the big metal keyboard in the sky ... he loved an inky ribbon.

It was so nice of Wee Allan's pal, Ross King MBE, to write the foreword. He's doing so well. He's doing so well. I watch him on Good Morning Britain and Lorraine every day. It's just so much fun guessing what colour his hair is going to be. If I was a few years younger, I'd sweep him off his feet.

I'd also like to thank my lovely Wee Book lady, Susan, who asked me to write this book in the first place. She has helped me so much and has given me so much encouragement.

And last but not least, I'd like to thank you all, my dear readers, for buying my book (mind, maybe you – yes, you! – found it in a loo somewhere).

Remember that if you ever need any advice on those wee problems that arise in life, all you have to do is write to me at the Edinburgh Bugle. I'm all ears, you know.

Right-oh ma darlings, I'm off noo. If you've enjoyed my book, tell your friends. If you haven't, shut yer mooth.

Love always,

Aunty M

The Wee Book Company

AWARD-WINNING INDEPENDENT PUBLISHER

The Wee Book o' Grannies' Sayin's
The Wee Book o' Pure Stoatin' Joy
The Wee Book o' Cludgie Banter
The Wee Book o' Winchin'
The Wee Book o' Napper Nippin' Puzzles
Ma Wee Book o' Gettin' Sh*te Done
Ma Wee Book o' Clarty Secrets
Big Tam's Kilted Wurkoots
If It's Broon It's Cooked, If It's Black It's Buggert
Bite Ma Scone
A Guy Scunnert Guide to the Nine to Five
Scotland's Witches and Wizards – Stranger Than Fiction
Arthur, the Sleepy Giant
Big Morag the Tartan Fairy

www.theweebookcompany.com

ANOTHER YUMPER

Love

Allan